Happy Birthday Earth

元気な地球
鈴木麻由　7才　　日本

Healthy Earth
Mayu Suzuki Japan

KIDS EARTH GALLERY編
メディアファクトリー

Dad was born on the Earth.
Mom was born on the Earth.
Grandpa and Grandma were born on the Earth.
I was born in Japan,
and Japan was born on the Earth.
United States, Soviet Union, Germany, China,
they are all children of Mother Earth.
So I'm her kid, aren't I?!
The Air, the water, the woods, the sea, the sky,
the Rainbow, the Typhoon, the word processor, the Otoshidama,
the hamburger, doggie John, birdie Piko, crawfish Ben,
the shoes, the scissors, the Tsukudani, they were
all born from Mother Earth.
The shiitake was also born from her.
Huh!! Mother Earth is great, isn't she?!
But dad told me
that
Mother Earth isn't fine......
I've asked dad if it is because of "the germ",
dad answered me that we have to be careful
not to become one of "the germ".

Happy Birthday Earth!

Please, get well soon.
Mom told me that I'll get sick if you won't recover......
Grandpa is in the garden and he's worried.
Grandma is in the Kotatsu and she's worried.
We are all worried for your health.
Please, get well soon.
I'll try to stop being fussy about what I eat.

Love from all of your kids.

Masashi Sada

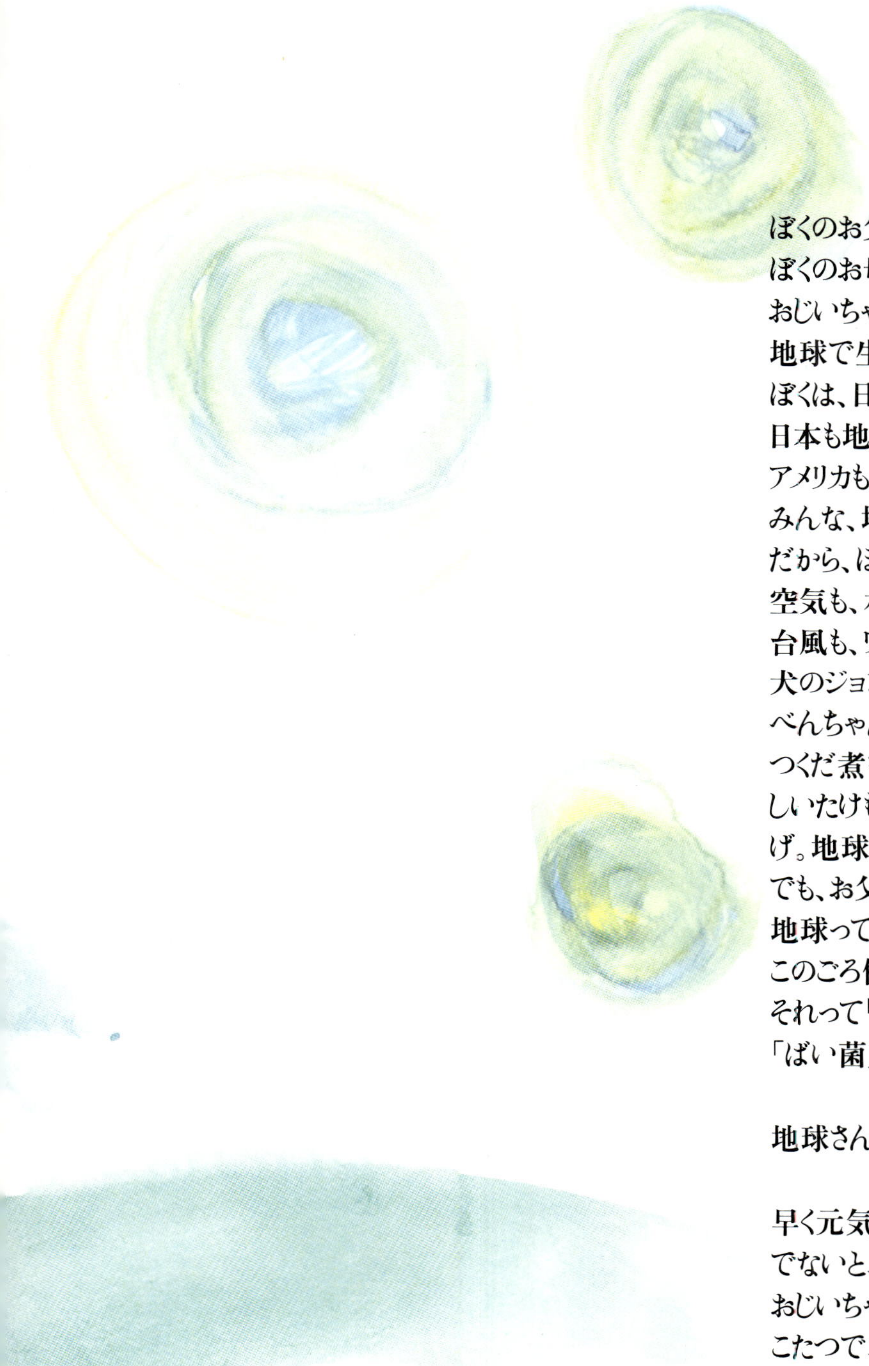

きれいな地球

坂本悦子　3才　　日本

Beautiful Means Earth

Etsuko Sakamoto　Japan

ぼくのお父さんは地球で生まれました。
ぼくのお母さんも地球で生まれました。
おじいちゃんも、おばあちゃんも、
地球で生まれました。
ぼくは、日本でうまれたのに、
日本も地球から生まれたそうです。
アメリカも、ソ連も、ドイツも中国も、
みんな、地球の子供なんだってね。
だから、ぼくも、地球の子供なんだ。
空気も、水も、森も、海も、空も、虹も、
台風も、ワープロも、お年玉も、ハンバーグも、
犬のジョンも、小鳥のピー子も、ザリガニの
べんちゃんも、くつや、ハサミや、
つくだ煮も、地球から生まれたんだって。
しいたけもだって。
げ。地球ってすげーじゃん。
でも、お父さんが言ってた。
地球って、
このごろ健康がすぐれないんだって。
それって「ばい菌」じゃないのって言ったら、
「ばい菌」にならないようにしようねって、お父さんが言いました。

地球さん、おたんじょう日おめでとう。

早く元気になってください。
でないと、ぼくも病気になっちゃうって、お母さんが言ってた。
おじいちゃんは庭で、おばあちゃんは、
こたつで、みんなしんぱいしてます。
元気になってね。
へんしょくやめますから

愛をこめて、　あなたのこどもたちより

さだまさし

Is it a helthy Earth?

登坂真巳　12才　日本

Mami Tosaka Japan

地球

アマド・ナセル　3才　パキスタン

The Earth

Ahmad Nasir　Pakistan

地球

アントニー・ランバート　2才　　フランス

The Earth

Antonie Lambert　France

その子のなまえ

太陽さん　太陽さん
あなたのこどもがヘンですよ

疲れてますよ　病気みたい
呼吸も乱れてるし　目もうつろ

救急車を呼んでください
その子のなまえは地球です

太陽さん　太陽さん
あなたのこどもがヘンですよ

朝倉　勇

THE CHILD IS ILL

Oh, my dear SUN
Your child looks ill

Listen, his hard breath
Look, his vacant eyes
He must be so tired, I'm sure

Call for the ambulance!
Tell them
His name is EARTH

Oh, my dear SUN
Your child looks ill

Isamu Asakura
Translation : Ayako Asakura, Kaoriko Asakura

空飛ぶ家
ヤイミ・モカ・ヴォルディスフィノ　8才　キューバ

A Flying House
Yaimi Moca Voldisfino Cuba

ハッピーバースデー

バーナデット・アップルキー　13才　　ベリンダ・イウェン　11才　　オーストラリア

Happy Birthday

Bernadette Applekee　Belinda Ewen　Australia

パッピーバースデー

メリッサ・ヤング　5才　　オーストラリア

Happy Birthday

Melissa Young　Australia

ハッピーバースデー

ファビアン・モローン　6才　　オーストラリア

Happy Birthday

Fabian Morrone　Australia

元気な地球

池田ユリ　6才　　日本

Healthy Earth

Yuri Ikeda Japan

MIKA SUGIYAMA
SEISEN-3B
AGE 8

Mika Sugiyama
3rd grade
Seisen Intl. School

10/7/90

Don't you think it's mean
Not to keep the earth clean
For all the human beans

Pick up all the trash
Don't do it just for cash
It can be done in a dash

You would be full of joy
Even if you are a little boy
Without a toy

You should help others
Without being told by mothers
So we'll feel like brothers

The heuman bean family

ヒューマン・ビーンズ

ねえ、ヒトのために
地球をよごしてしまうのって
はずかしいことだって思わない？

ゴミをみんなひろいましょ。
お金のためだけにするんじゃなくってね。
あっという間にできちゃうんだから。

あなたも　きっときっと　うれしさでいっぱいになるわ。
たとえあなたが
おもちゃをもっていない男の子だとしてもね。

他の人のおてつだいをしましょ。
お母さんにいいつけられなくてもね。
そうすれば、私たち　きっときっと　キョウダイになれるわ。

杉山ミカ　8歳　　日本

『ちょうちょ』

ちょうちょは　地球の風を感じている。
かすかな風に乗って　お空の散歩。
お友達をたくさんつくって　地球の風を描いている。

小川朝子

"Butterfly"

The Butterfly feels the wind of the Earth.
She goes for a fly on the slight soft wind.
She's got new friends and
She paints the wind of the earth with them.

Asako Ogawa

空を飛ぶチョウチョ号
永井　萌　4才　　日本

Butterfly

Moe Nagai　Japan

新年の朝

アンナ・アガルコバ　9才　　バヴェル・ヴォドロフスキー　8才
ソビエト

The Morning of the New Year

Anna Agarkova　Paval Vodolazskii　U.S.S.R.

泣きたいみたい

あの子　泣いてるみたい
どこか　ぐあいがわるいみたい
地球みたい
なのに　いろんなこと知ってるみたい
でも　わからないみたい
なら　アホみたい
みんなこまってるみたい
たすけてほしいみたい
さけびたいみたい
でも　どうしていいかわからないみたい
まいごのこどもみたい
泣きたいみたい　地球みたい

朝倉　勇

About to cry

She looks like crying
She looks like suffering
Just like the earth

She seems to know everything
But without understanding
just like a fool

"What shall we do?
She needs help
She is about to cry
What can we do?"

She looks like a lost child
Just like the earth

Isamu Asakura
Translation : Ayako Asakura, Kaoriko Asakura

かわいそうな地球

坂本彩子　8才　日本

Poor Earth

Ayako Sakamoto　Japan

もっといい地球にしようよ

サーディア・ナセル　9才　　パキスタン

Make a Better Earth

Seadia Nasir　Pakistan

So much trash did I see as
I walked towards the sea.
Paper, cigarette butts
And lots more—
Even an apple core.
Trash transforms the world
into a filthy ball.
Since God created this world
for us all to enjoy.
Shouldn't we be ashamed
at all?

Ethel Seno

海の方へむかって歩いていったら、
たくさんのゴミを僕は見ちゃったよ。
紙、タバコ、丸太、他にもたくさん…
リンゴのしんまで落ちていた…
ゴミは、世界を　ただのきたないボールにしちゃうのに、
神様は、僕らが楽しめるようにと
この世界を　つくって下さったのに
はずかしいと全く思わなくてもいいのかなあ。

エセル　セノ

地球をきれいにして

ダイアナ・ブルックス　9才　　アメリカ

Make the Earth Beautiful

Diana Brooks　U.S.A

地球にやさしい乗り物

安藤井達　7才　　日本

A Kind Machine

Seita Ando Japan

There isn't a Crocodile Ecologist
not a Lion, not a Tiger,
and maybe not a pink strange mammal.
Body is more important than words for them,
'cause they are the most natural thing for them.

When I went to see the Kinoshita Circus
I talked with an old clown
"Being on a rolling ball means balance."
he laughted on the rolling ball standing on his hand.
"It's important feeling to be tied with the ball."

We are all on a big rolling ball
like animals let's try to be on it nicely
almost to forget that we're on the ball.

Shinji Ishii

わににエコロジストはいない。
らいおんにも、とらにも。
たぶん、ピンクの妙なホニュー類にも。
彼らにしてみれば言葉より、まず体。
彼ら自身が自然なわけやから。

木下大サーカスを見に行った時に、
じーさんピエロの話を聞いた。
「玉のりはな、バランスや。」
片手で逆立ちしながら、じじーは玉の上で笑った。
「玉と自分がつながる感じが大切やな。」

ぼく達はみんな壮大な玉のりをしている。
けもの達のように、
美しく玉にのろう。
玉にのっていることを
ほとんど忘れんばかりに。

石井慎二

地球にやさしい乗り物

志村　星　6才　日本

Kind Machines

Sei Shimura Japan

小さな手

花をにぎって手をあげる
天にとどくのは小さな手

大きな手には花はない
その手はおかねをにぎってる

笛をふくのは小さな手
きいた地球がにっこりする

大きな手は銃をうつ
そのおとで地球がこわれてく

朝倉　勇

ONE TINY HAND

One tiny hand
If with a flower
It'll reach high in the sky

One big hand
Not with a flower
But with money, yes, eagerly

One tiny hand
When plays the flute
It makes the earth smile and happy

One big hand
When fires a shot
It makes the earth break and painfully

Isamu Asakura
Translation : Ayako Asakura, Kaoriko Asakura

一輪の花だけじゃ生け花はできない

M・スミルノフスキー　11才　　ソビエト

Only One Flower is No Good for Ikebana

M.Smirnovsky　U.S.S.R.

リーナー・メレラ・ハデッツ　9才　キューバ
Reinier Merera Hdez　Cuba

カブト虫はカブト虫色
空は空色
木立ちは木立ち色
葉は葉色
魚は魚色
花びらは花びら色
山は山色
太陽は太陽色
羽根は羽根色

まいこちゃんの
クレヨンが
たりなくなりました

長薗安浩

The Beetle is beetle color
The Sky is sky color
The Grove is grove color
A Leaf is leaf color
The Fish is fish color
A Petal is petal color
The Mountain is mountain color
The Sun is sun color
A Feather is feather color

And now Maiko has used up her crayon.

Yasuhiro Nagazono

元気な地球

持田麻衣子　12才　日本

Healthy Earth

Maiko Mochida Japan

子供たちの絵で地球を塗りかえよう

「地球が元気でいられるようにお誕生日をつくってみんなでプレゼントをしよう」と、志村　星（6才）のアイディアでキッズ・アース・ギャラリーはスタートしました。

地球にやさしい気持ちを、アート（ハート）にした作品を世界中の子供たちから集めています。

わたしたちは、地球という大きなお家に住む家族の一員です。世界中のお友達で力を合わせて、わたしたちの大切な地球を守っていきましょう。

子供たちのアート（ハート）は、どれもみな、パワフルで夢と希望にあふれています。純粋で美しい心を持つ子供たちの作品は、見る人すべてに感動を与えます。子供の持つ創造性は、大人の何倍も心にうったえる力を持っているのです。子供たちの心が一つになり、やさしさで、美しく平和な地球に塗りかえれば、大人は必ずそれに目を開きます。大人に教えてもらうのではなく、逆に大人に教えてあげることもできます。このキッズパワーで、わたしたちの星である地球を、もっと住みやすくすることができるのです。

子供は地球アーティスト。21世紀は、今の子供たちが担います。地球アーティストのやさしい心と、希望にあふれた作品を絵本にして、世界中のいろいろな人たちに見てもらいたい。そしたら、ずーっと元気な地球に住めるメッセージになります。わたしたちは、子供たちに輝きと自信を与えることができます。そして、この絵本は永遠に続く、わたしたちの星、地球への贈物です。

キッズ・アース・ギャラリー代表　志村晴美

Repainting the Earth With Children's Drawings

The idea for KIDS EARTH GALLERY came from Sei Shimura, age 6. He suggested giving the earth a birthday, with presents, to keep it happy. Inspired, we began collecting artwork (heartwork) from all over the world made by children who love Mother Earth.

In this great big home called 'Earth', each one of us is but a single member of the global family. We can protect our precious planet by pooling our efforts and energy as worldwide friends.

Kids' artwork (heartwork) is rich and powerful, overflowing with hopes and dreams. Each viewer cannot help but feel moved by the sight of these works, drawn from the pure and lovely minds of the children.

In connecting with the heart, the imagination of a child far surpasses that of grown-ups. Adults are sure to open up their eyes to the ideas of children who repaint a peaceful earth in the beautiful colors of love and kindness. Rather than learning from their elders, on the contrary, children have an important message to teach - Tapping Kids' Power can make our planet Earth a better place to live.

The children of today will carry us into the 21st century. In making this children's picture book, we hope people worldwide will be touched by the children, the Earth Artists, whose minds and hearts are filled with love and hope. Their message to the world: WE WANT TO LIVE ON A HEALTHY, HAPPY PLANET!

We want our children to be able to face the future with confidence and brightness. May the spirit of this book continue throughout eternity: This is our gift to planet Earth.

Director of KIDS EARTH GALLERY Harumi Shimura

Happy Birthday Earth　1991年4月1日　初版第1刷発行

編者　*KIDS EARTH GALLERY*
発行者　株式会社 メディアファクトリー
編集部　販売部
東京都港区浜松町1-18-16 住友浜松町ビル　〒105
電話 03-5472-2454(代表)
印刷所
製本所　株式会社 精興社

ISBN4-88991-214-2 C0740
落丁本･乱丁本はお取替え致します。
定価はカバーに表示してあります。

STAFF

Planning	*KIDS EARTH GALLERY* メディアファクトリー
Art Direction	サカグチケン ファクトリー
Photographer	稲富　均
Producer	藤原　和博
Editors	松川　恵巳 鈴木　美佐子
Transrator	杉崎　リカ
Special Thanks	朝倉　勇 朝倉　文子 朝倉　香子 石井　慎二 小川　朝子 鎌田　宏之 さだ　まさし 長薗　安浩 クリエイションギャラリー

地球さん　おたんじょう日おめでとう
志村　星　6才　日本

Happy Birthday Earth
Sei Shimura　Japan